Zoo Animals

I0813866

TIGERS AT THE ZOO

By Seth Lynch

Please visit our website, www.garethstevens.com. For a free color catalog of all our high-quality books, call toll free 1-800-542-2595 or fax 1-877-542-2596.

Library of Congress Cataloging-in-Publication Data

Names: Lynch, Seth, author.
Title: Tigers at the zoo / Seth Lynch.
Description: New York : Gareth Stevens Publishing, [2020] | Series: Zoo animals | Includes index.
Identifiers: LCCN 2018039585| ISBN 9781538239506 (paperback) | ISBN 9781538239520 (library bound) | ISBN 9781538239513 (6 pack)
Subjects: LCSH: Tiger–Juvenile literature. | Zoo animals–Juvenile literature.
Classification: LCC QL737.C23 L945 2020 | DDC 599.756–dc23
LC record available at https://lccn.loc.gov/2018039585

First Edition

Published in 2020 by
Gareth Stevens Publishing
111 East 14th Street, Suite 349
New York, NY 10003

Copyright © 2020 Gareth Stevens Publishing

Editor: Therese Shea
Designer: Katelyn E. Reynolds

Photo credits: Cover, p. 1 Mati Nitibhon/Shutterstock.com; p. 5 iyd39/Shutterstock.com; p. 7 IgorBratyshko/Shutterstock.com; p. 9 sittitap/Shutterstock.com; p. 11 (top left) Eric Isselee/Shutterstock.com; p. 11 (top right) Popova Valeriya/Shutterstock.com; p. 11 (bottom left) Matt Gibson/Shutterstock.com; p. 11 (bottom right) Gwoeii/Shutterstock.com; pp. 13, 24 (stripe) Pontus Edenberg/Shutterstock.com; p. 15 Louis W/Shutterstock.com; p. 17 Ondrej Prosicky/Shutterstock.com; p. 19 Sarosh Lodhi/Shutterstock.com; pp. 21, 24 (cubs) otsphoto/Shutterstock.com; p. 23 M. Robbemont/Shutterstock.com.

All rights reserved. No part of this book may be reproduced in any form without permission in writing from the publisher, except by a reviewer.

Printed in the United States of America

CPSIA compliance information: Batch #CS19GS: For further information contact Gareth Stevens, New York, New York at 1-800-542-2595.

Contents

I see tigers at the zoo.
I learn a lot!

Tigers are
the largest cats.

Tigers live in Asia.

There are five kinds of tigers.

Most have dark stripes.

Some tigers
are white!

Tigers like to live alone.

They hunt at night.
They eat meat.

Tiger babies
are called cubs.

Tiger cubs play!
I like the tigers
at the zoo!

Words to Know

cubs

stripe

Index